A Girl With Healing Words

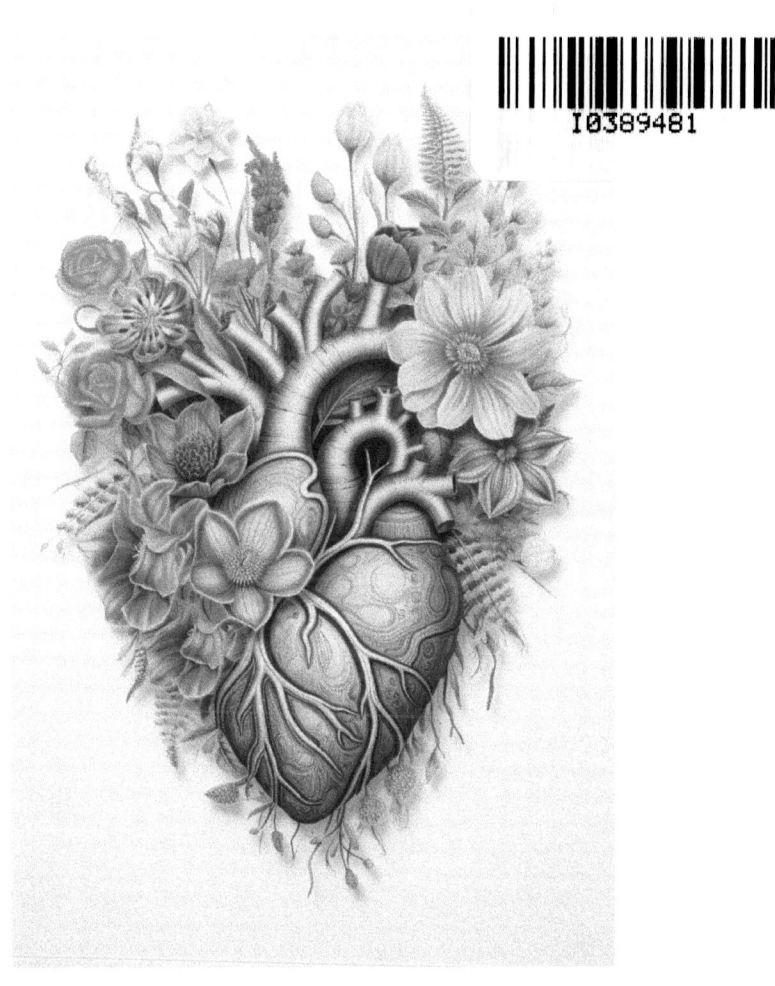

A Collection of Poems by Carmen Sydney

A Girl With Healing Words

Copyright © 2023 by Carmen Johnson

Printed in the Unites States of America

Published by
Kingdom Publishing, LLC
Odenton, Maryland

All rights reserved. No part of this book may be reproduced or transmitted in any form or by any means, electronic or mechanical, including photocopying, recording or by any information storage and retrieval system without written permission from the author, except for the inclusion of brief quotations in a review.

ISBN: 978-1-947741-87-4

Table of Contents

Poem #1
Resurrection
7

Poem #2
God Hears
13

Poem #3
Friend's Soulmates
17

Poem #4
Cycles
21

Poem #5
My One Sweet Love
25

Poem #6
Healing is NOT Linear
29

Poem #7
Step into Your Purpose
31

Poem #8
Acceptance is the First Step
33

Poem #9
Daily Thanksgiving
35

Poem #10
Faithful Love
37

Poem #11
He Commands
39

Poem #12
God is Love
41

Poem #13
Is God Disappointed?
43

Poem 14
All About Me Now
45

Poem #15
Walking on Glass
47

Poem #16
Variety of Tears
53

Poem #17
Love Languages
57

Preface

My inspiration for this collection of poems comes from my traumatic life experiences. It is my goal to help others heal and find solace through poetry. I pray that readers are comforted by my words and by knowing that they are not alone. This book is to inspire and give hope to the wounded and brokenhearted. You are heard and seen by our Lord and Saviour Jesus Christ.

Lord my God, I called to you for help, and you healed me.

Psalm 30:2

Poem #1

Resurrection

The resurrection.
It is not an event to be celebrated.
It is a man that elevated.
The sun of the infinite divine God
that rose and levitated.
The one that was a perfect sacrifice for a death that
couldn't be emancipated,
At least not by mankind.
The one who had authority to make the blind see,
Save the ones in need,
Make disease flee,
Find the live sheep
and set the ones in bondage sin free.
The name is Jesus,
King of the Jews.
His birth started time, so what does that tell you?
Ministered for three years even though people refused,
Showed many signs and people still acted
like they had no clue.
I mean, who knew that God loved us so much that
sending his one and only son would be for you,

—A Girl with Healing Words—

He sent out his word and healed them; he rescued them from the grave.

Psalm 107:20

Or even for a second chance.
Wanting a relationship, restless nights,
and pursuing the Father's plan.
Coming down and being fully God and fully man,
Begging you to take his hand.
Hold on, I know this lifetime may be hard
but it's better if you give him a chance.
He knows your pain.
He knows your shame.
He knows what it's like to be humiliated and blamed.
He knows the world will hate you because of his name.
He knew it wasn't a mistake to give you salvation,
mercy, and grace.
So each whip that tore his flesh,
Each hit that brought him closer to death,
The crown of thorns around his head
Mocked, spit on, tormented,
profound nails on each wrist.
Hung up like a discomfit
And through his bloody eyes
and with each breath of pain,
The last three words "It is finished"
The beginning of change.
He knew it was worth it.
He knew it was worth it.
Cause on the third day all the earth would shake.

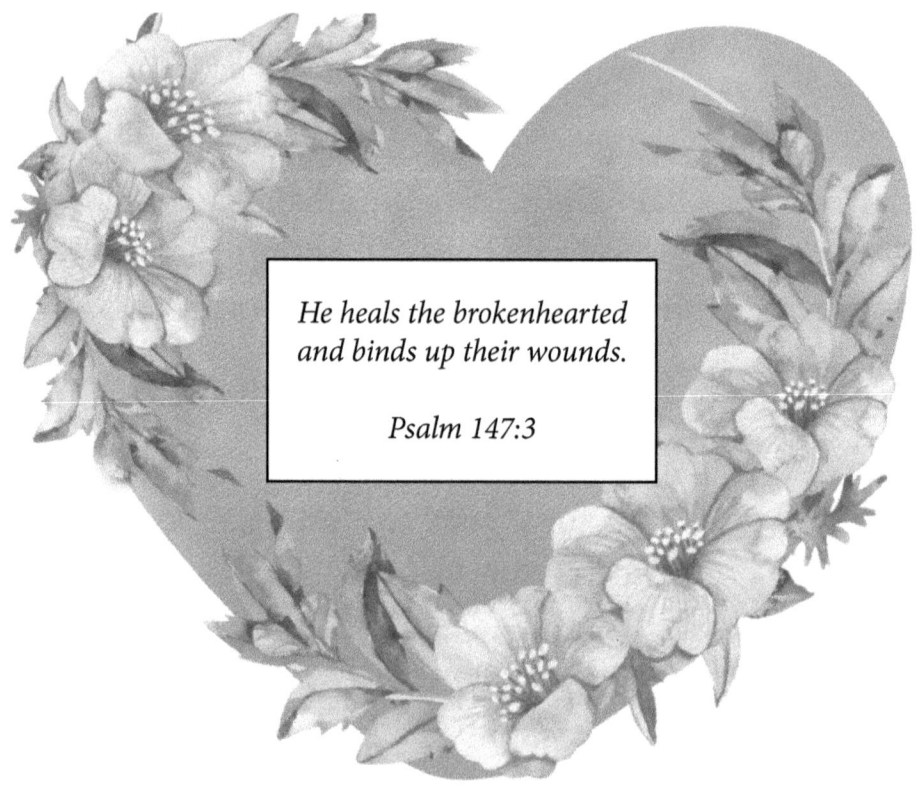

*He heals the brokenhearted
and binds up their wounds.*

Psalm 147:3

They would see that the Messiah, the King of kings
could not be kept in a death state.
They would see that he has the keys of Calvary.
They would see that he is the Risen King.
Death has no sting
Rejoice cause we serve a God of Victory.
Defeat cannot be in your vocabulary
Lost should not be in your dictionary.
We serve a God that went to hell and back because He
believes we were worthy.
We serve a God death cannot hold down
because he is mighty.
I am the daughter of royalty and if he stands with me
then who can defeat me.
And how can I lose if he already has the victory.
So I will tell the world
My God is the Risen King.
My God died for me.
And my God is the Resurrection.
So, no the resurrection is not an event.
It is a person.
Jesus.

He gives strength to the weary and increases the power of the weak.

Isaiah 40:29

Poem #2

God Hears

If I am sad, do I just pray about it?
If my mental health is off, do I pray about it?
If I sit in my room, and cry all night
Do I just pray about it?
To all my brothers and sisters under the Lord
I ask
If I am depressed
Do I pray about it?
I sit in my room alone and wonder
"If I pray about it, will it go away?"
The question in wonder
Will it go away?
Other followers call it demons
Yet, I call it a human emotion.
Emotions all life shares.
I ask of it
If you are sad.
Do more than just pray...
Cry every single emotion you have, as you have soul
for the night, you are a human being, as all of life
carries emotion

Heal me, Lord, and I will be healed; save me and I will be saved, for you are the one I praise.

Jeremiah 17:14

I give you my ears, shall I hear your cries
I give you my eyes, as I see your tears
I give you love and care, must you feel attention once more I give you my heart, shall my heart find yours
I give you my soul.
Must I apologize to those
who look away from your pain
Must you not suffer anymore
Cry no more
As God may guide you on a path of righteousness
Express the truth of mind
Must a true follower show you grace and humanity
Pray for it, shall he do his works
Ask of it, must we stand hand in hand
May God bless you.

Nevertheless, I will bring health and healing to it; I will heal my people and will let them enjoy abundant peace and security.

Jeremiah 33:6

Poem #3

Friend's Soulmates

I want to string together the prettier words for you
in hopes of fully conveying the depth of my gratitude.
To have you in my life, is a true blessing
that was never—disguised.
You entered my life with grace as if
you already knew
you were the missing part in my life,
the other half I desperately needed.
For the longest time,
I thought friendship was a casual affair.
Not something you put your heart and soul into.
It came and went, no need for a ritualistic morning,
or it was something wretched and burdensome,
carrying all the problems of others before
sinking into welcomed solitude.
Yet now it feels impossible to bear a day alone,
unless there is the promise of
talking to you afterward.
You will forever be a part of my heart and soul,
and the feeling will strengthen over time,
and it is impossible to fully describe how pure it is,

He will wipe every tear from their eyes. There will be no more death' or mourning or crying or pain, for the old order of things has passed away.

Revelation 21:4

how lucky I am——
to be so comfortable with someone
that you consider them your second half.

—A Girl with Healing Words—

Gracious words are a honeycomb, sweet to the soul and healing to the bones.

Proverbs 16:24

Poem #4

Cycles

I'm stopping the cycle this time
I know in your mind you believe you
have one more time, because I was
kind enough to let you believe it, but
this time is different.
I feel it in my gut.
This time I know who you are
so I expect nothing different
because the last time you told me
I just decided not to listen.
You see, it was never you I couldn't stop talking to.
The problem was me.
You see, I have this overwhelming thing
that I can't seem to beat called "attachment."
So, sorry if I went against everything I told you
cause I've been psychoanalyzing myself
and I realized there are a lot of things
I haven't dealt with.
So, when you told me that
you'd do things that you never do, it only reminded
me of all of my daddy issues

Peace, I leave with you; my peace I give you. I do not give to you as the world gives. Do not let your hearts be troubled and do not be afraid.

John 14:27

and now here I am feeling
used and abused and it only makes me
pull away from you because
it reminded me of everything he would do.
So, when I say that you're not special, I mean that.
Only thing special to me is
someone finally being everything that you and him
couldn't be.
So, I'm stopping the cycle this time.
It's not that I need to heal,
I just need to deal with all of these feels
that's keeping me on a wheel of toxicity.
So don't think I'm delusional,
I'm just attached to you, that's all.
But, once the problem dissolves,
I won't be at your every beck and call
and you won't hear from me at all because
I'm stopping the cycle this time.

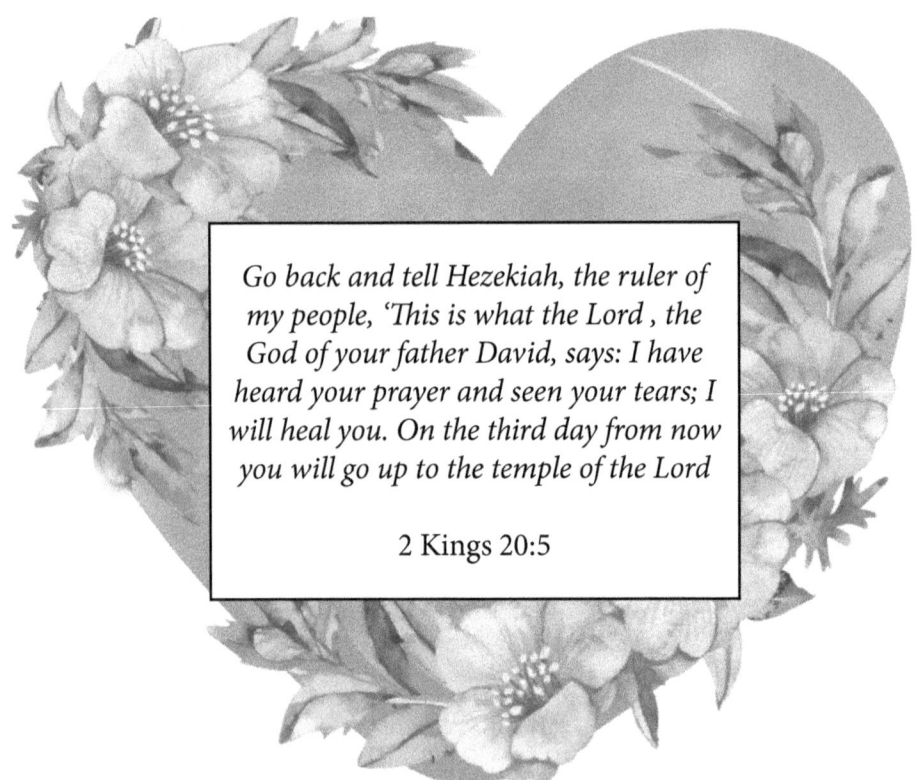

Go back and tell Hezekiah, the ruler of my people, 'This is what the Lord, the God of your father David, says: I have heard your prayer and seen your tears; I will heal you. On the third day from now you will go up to the temple of the Lord

2 Kings 20:5

Poem #5

My One Sweet Love

"My little sunshine, my only sunshine."
Those sweet six words you used to say.
"You make me happy when skies are grey"
Eight words I can't even bring myself to say.
Since you are now gone, I'm so lost.
I'm missing you more and more every day.
My one sweet love.
I've accomplished so much with a smile on my face.
Time and time again, my skies are still grey.
Those short five years, you spent with me every day
Without you here, I'm at distraught
But, I'm your little sunshine, your only sunshine
At least I thought.
I cannot blame you for what has happened.
Which is why,
I pray.
I pray day in and day out.
My one sweet love.
I will continue to push on.
Just how you did.
You were one strong soul which is what everyone said.

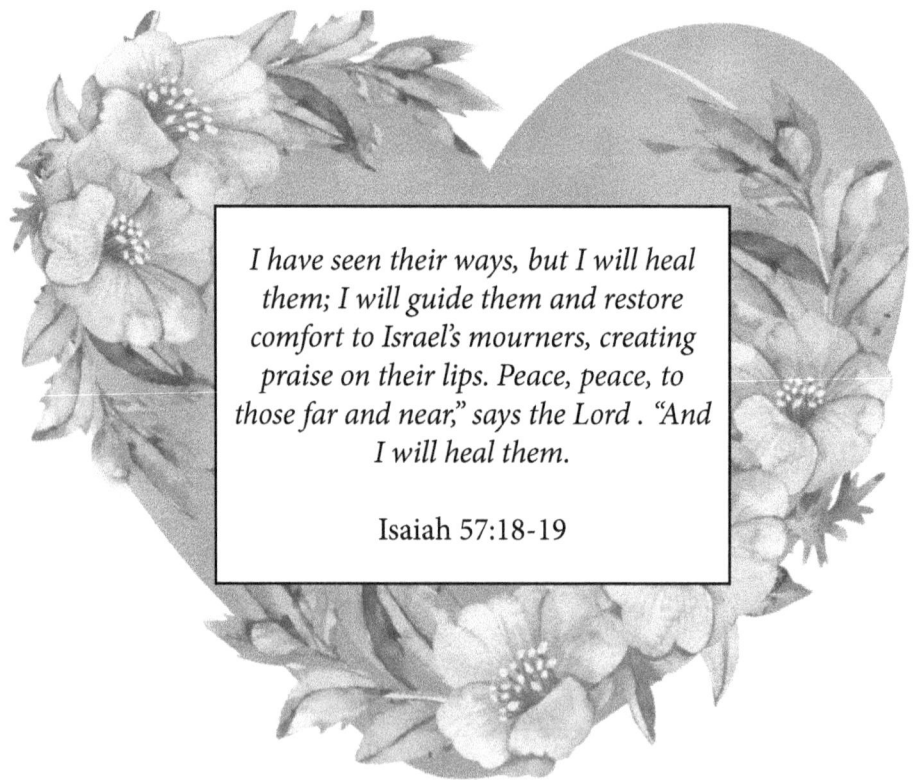

I have seen their ways, but I will heal them; I will guide them and restore comfort to Israel's mourners, creating praise on their lips. Peace, peace, to those far and near," says the Lord . "And I will heal them.

Isaiah 57:18-19

I pray to see you in another lifetime.
God, gives his toughest battles to his strongest soldiers.
Well, It's been 12 years and I'm still clashing through
Trying to make it out alive
to conquer and defend.
Only for you my one sweet love.
Because I'm your sunshine and only sunshine.

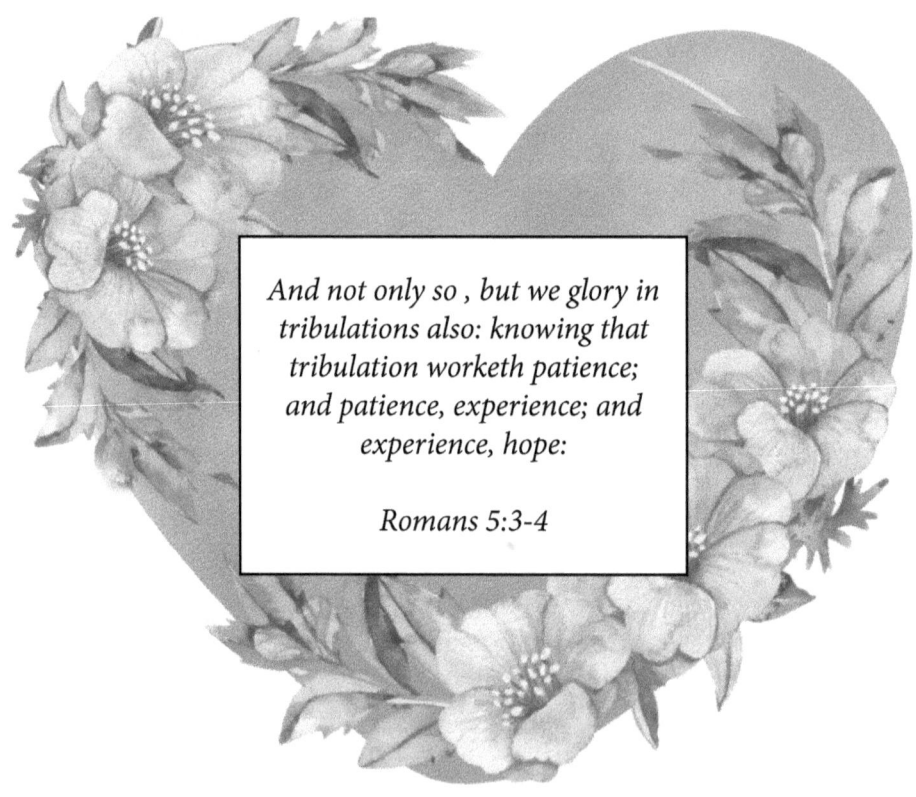

And not only so, but we glory in tribulations also: knowing that tribulation worketh patience; and patience, experience; and experience, hope:

Romans 5:3-4

Poem #6

Healing is NOT Linear

The flowers are starting to bloom again
And so am I.
Nothing is permanent
Enough to hurt me
Forever.
The bliss feeling of taking a deep breath,
Spring air filling my lungs
I know I'll be better.

—A Girl with Healing Words—

*The righteous cry out, and the LORD hears them;
he delivers them from all their troubles.*

Psalm 34:17

Poem #7

Step Into Your Purpose

Be a healer.
You're mad.
He is your provider, let him give you rest.
If you trust God's process
You will see trials and storms are only tests.
But if spiritual works that comes with this
army of bad spirits,
thinking it will leave a negative effect.
You better not serve hell cause God
has not failed you yet.
Strap yourself with the forearm of God
and let him use you.
Cause when you serve the Lord Almighty
you will never lose.
No disease, no weapon formed against you
shall conquer you.
You better step into your purpose,
cause it was made for you.

*The LORD is close to the brokenhearted
and saves those who are crushed in spirit.*

Psalm 34:18

Poem #8

Acceptance is the First Step

Sometimes you just have to be at peace with the world
And accept the way things are
To come to terms with the impending battles
And the things that have potential
To make them that much harder.
Grant yourself acceptance
Whether or not the outcome is in your favor
Everything happens for a reason
And there's no point fighting for something
Destined to escape.

> The righteous person may have many troubles, but the LORD delivers him from them all.
>
> Psalm 34:19

Poem #9

Daily Thanksgiving

There is power in gratitude
In regular negative situations.
So, let me go first
Thank you Lord for saving me
For singleness and goal-oriented
For going through the hardest battles
To get closer to you.
Thank you for letting people leave
And leaving me with loyal friends.
For taking loved ones to Heaven,
And allowing me not to take life for granted.
Thank you for the rain
And the tears
But also for the sun
And laughter,
I'm grateful to experience
A transformed mind
And seek for Kingdom
In Heaven and on earth.

—A Girl with Healing Words—

Be gracious to me, O Lord, for I am languishing; heal me, O Lord, for my bones are troubled.

Psalm 6:2

Poem #10

Faithful Love

Why do I rush my life when
Christ took his tender time with it?
Shouldn't I be rejoicing in that?
He is so deliberate, so intentional, and so patient.
He wants to love me forever.
He wants surrendered hearts for the long haul.
Now is my only chance to trust him with
true faith—I don't want to miss out on that.

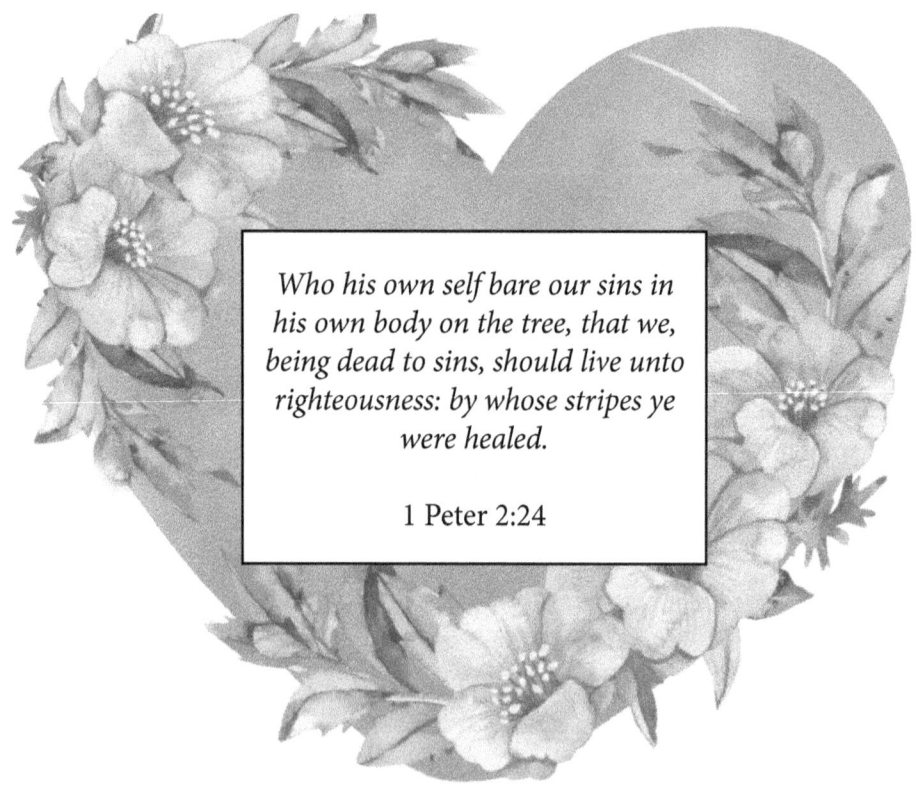

Who his own self bare our sins in his own body on the tree, that we, being dead to sins, should live unto righteousness: by whose stripes ye were healed.

1 Peter 2:24

Poem #11

He Commands

His very first command was
to be fruitful and increase.
So who am I to sit on all the gifts
and talents he gave me?
I'm taking back and multiplying everything
I ever let the enemy steal from me.
So everybody connected to me
is gonna see God's glory.
That's the type of faith
that's going to make the earth shake.
That's the type of faith
I need all day every day.

Whoever believes in the Son has eternal life, but whoever rejects the Son will not see life, for God's wrath remains on them.

John 3:36

Poem #12

God is Love

Teach others what it really means.
God is love and a sacrifice.
He knew only the death of his son
would bring us peace,
and tranquility, and set us free.
He knew there would be no progression
without pain.
And let them put him in chains
Because he would rather see us saved
and give us grace.
And I would rather choose God
over anything any day.

We demolish arguments and every pretension that sets itself up against the knowledge of God, and we take captive every thought to make it obedient to Christ.

2 Corinthians 10:5

Poem #13

Is God Disappointed?

It's not like God is bothered
by not having my full attention.
It's fine anyways,
I'll save it for the next Christian.
The next person who's actually up for the mission.
The next person who will worship genuinely
and not pretend.
You know, the ones who clap and Amen.
Then moments after blast YB in the Benz.
But, I'm no better I'm no different.
How can I worship and hold onto
anger and unforgiveness?
How am I supposed to give reverence
to the same person I'm blaming?
How am I supposed to worship God
if we're not intimate?
How am I supposed to surrender my all
when I'm so used
to disappointment?

You, dear children, are from God and have overcome them, because the one who is in you is greater than the one who is in the world.

1 John 4:4

Poem #14

All About Me Now

I have made a choice to wash my hands
with everything that no longer serves me.
No matter how close you may be
nothing or no one is worth my sanity.
I am evolving and growing into
the woman that I want to be, that I am eager to be.
So, why would I let you be in the way of my dreams?
Infectious bacteria has no name here
not in my heart and certainly isn't worth my tears.
It's so hard to control my emotions when
I was taught to be nothing but, compassionate.
They never told me that I was the one
that they would try to take advantage of and
jerk around like hand me downs.
When is the good part coming?
Where is my gold crown?

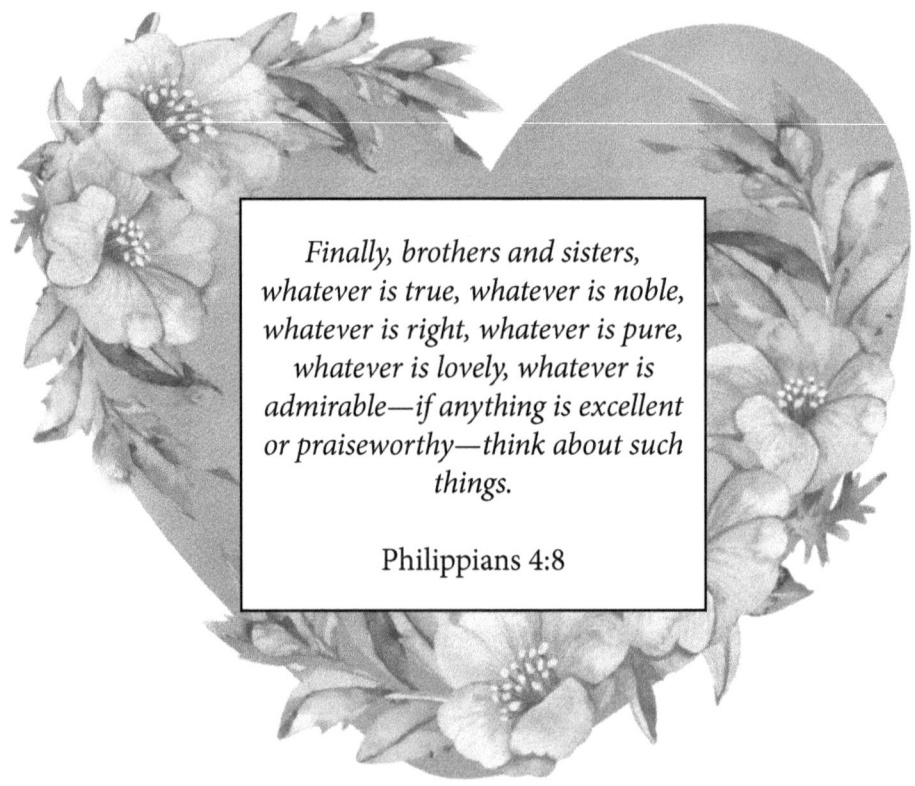

Finally, brothers and sisters, whatever is true, whatever is noble, whatever is right, whatever is pure, whatever is lovely, whatever is admirable—if anything is excellent or praiseworthy—think about such things.

Philippians 4:8

Poem #15

Walking on Glass

You know, those friends
that you become strangely close with really fast.
But something in your heart tells you that there's
no chance it will last, because the entire thing
was simply too good to be true.
And this person is now someone who knows
everything you've ever gone through.
But this fact isn't bad in it of itself, it's almost like
the pain of putting a good book back up on it's shelf.
Except the pages are now torn
and some are even missing.
Just like a part of yourself is regretfully wishing that
you never opened up to them in the first place, as they
now know too much and it's backfiring in your face.
You put too much in and it took too much out of you.
People told you it's one-sided and now
you're finally seeing how it's true.
But, the act of leaving seems harder than staying
because, you have to admit the thought of losing them
is weighing heavily down on your mind
and on your heart,

—A Girl with Healing Words—

For the Spirit God gave us does not make us timid, but gives us power, love and self-discipline.

2 Timothy 1:7

even though you know you guys are better off apart.
It felt as if you were fighting for something
they never thought worth fighting for.
They put in the bare minimum
and you always put in way more.
This toxicity undeniably went both ways.
Neither were good for the other,
and yet both have always stayed.
Everything's a competition and words
tore each other down.
Things indirectly said would
trigger all of the breakdowns.
And it felt as if every single day,
you were walking on eggshells.
And, I hate to say it,
but maybe it is time for the final farewells.
Because it's not eggshells anymore.
It's moved to broken glass.
And the cuts on your feet are signs
that it's just not going to pass.
Some people are simply just not compatible
or meant to be friends.
The saying is literally all good things
must come to an end.
Everything seems to have
an underlying motive or reasoning

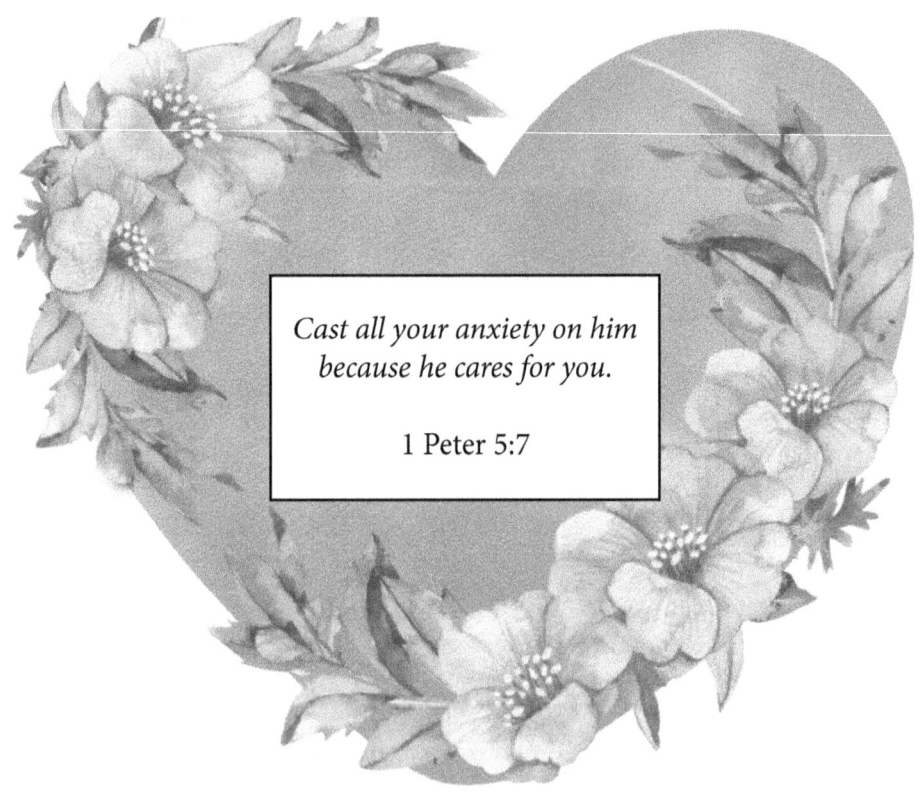

Cast all your anxiety on him because he cares for you.

1 Peter 5:7

because they come out stronger
from my own weakening.
Opinions start to differ solely to not agree.
And people on the outside start to tell you what they
see because they know that you deserve so much better.
But they'll indirectly tell you, maybe send a text or a letter,
because they know that you need to come to the
conclusion on your own.
That this friendship is harmful and this person is no
longer your home.
So, as you take another step along the shattered glass,
along the floor, you are walking away from the hurt,
the heartache, and more.
And, I promise, I know you're in agonizing pain.
But losing this one person opens the door for so many
others to gain the wonderful, selfless,
deserving girl that you are.
That you won't even notice,
the bloody cuts on your feet have faded to a scar.
And this scar will never fade, it acts as a lesson
for every, toxic relationship has made a lasting
impression.
But, it has led you to happiness and the genuine
friendships you now see loud and clear.
And the broken glass and bloody footprints
on the floor are just the paths that led you here.

For we live by faith, not by sight.

2 Corinthians 5:7

Poem #16

Variety of Tears

I have a variety of tears.
You know
You got the ones that you try to
choke back
You make that little noise in the
back of your throat
While you put your hand over your mouth
Squeeze your eyes shut
In hope that the tears stop
But they don't
And your body starts to shake
From all that hurt trying to come out
But you shake your head and say
Don't you make a sound
And you know you got that
other one
That comes out when you get to
thinking about all that hurt
Your eyes get red
start to blink real fast
You try to speak but your throat is on fire

Do not let your hearts be troubled. You believe in God; believe also in me.

John 14:1

And you ball up your fists
While your eyes start
to get blurry
And you lean your head back
so the tears won't fall
And you think to yourself
When did I become so weak
And of course, you can't forget the ones
That you try to hide
With all your power
And all your strength
But then that first tear slips out
And it's like all the other ones are trying
to catch up to it
And your chest
Someone's sitting on it
And the best thing you know
You can't breathe
You're on the floor
Begging for everything to stop
Just for a second
And you ask yourself
How am I going to make it?
I got a variety of tears
And each day I say
Hmm..Which one will it be today?

—A Girl with Healing Words—

My flesh and my heart may fail, but God is the strength of my heart and my portion forever.

Psalm 73:26

Poem #17

Love Languages

I want a communicative love.
That I'll give you all the five love languages
type of love.
Reassurance on a bad day, words of affirmation
type of love.
I'm proud, thankful, and grateful for you,
type of love
I want to be taken out for a picnic and prayer date,
a quality time
type of love.
Keeping God forefront and center
type of love.
Giving me the strength to get closer to our father
type of love.
We interlocking hands to pray.
That's a physical touch
type of love.
Gifting each other with Bibles,
oh that's an act of service
type of love.
I want all five love languages
type of love.

Why are you troubled? And why do thoughts arise in your hearts?

Luke 24:38

www.ingramcontent.com/pod-product-compliance
Lightning Source LLC
Chambersburg PA
CBHW041132110526
44592CB00020B/2779